Contents

The reptile house

Reptiles are scaly-skinned, "cold-blooded" creatures with a bony skeleton and a backbone. They live on land, in fresh water, and in the sea. The world is home to about 6 500 different reptile **species**. Scientists divide these into four main groups.

desert tortoise

Reptiles with shells

Tortoises, turtles and terrapins are known as Chelonians. All members of this group have a body that is protected by a shell. Tortoises live on land. Turtles and terrapins live in the sea or in rivers and ponds.

Snakes and lizards

The Squamata order contains every type of lizard and snake. It is by far the largest group of living reptiles. Amazingly, nearly all reptiles are lizards and snakes.

Snakes have no legs, so they get around by wrigglin

Armour-plated reptiles

Crocodiles, alligators, caimans, and gharials all belong to a group of reptiles called Crocodylia. Most live in warm freshwater rivers, lakes, and swamps. They have tough skin covering their whole bodies like armour.

crocodiles

Beak-head reptiles

The fourth group of reptiles only has one member! Tuataras look like lizards. However, unlike lizards, they have a bony arch over their eyes. This is why they are called "beak heads". Tuataras are only found in New Zealand.

their bodies.

COLD BLOOD

Reptiles are known as cold-blooded creatures, but they do not always have chilly blood. An animal is "cold-blooded" if its body temperature changes depending on how hot or cold the surroundings are. Reptiles **bask** in sunlight to heat up. If a reptile's body is not warm enough, its stomach cannot **digest** its food properly.

A tale of scales

Reptile skin is covered in overlapping, waterproof plates called scales. This layer of skin is good at keeping **moisture** inside, so that reptiles can survive in hot, dry places.

snake

caiman

skink
(a lizard)

tortoise

Sensible outfits

Skinks and snakes have smooth, flexible scales for burrowing or moving across ground. The leathery scales of caimans are strengthened by bony plates on the back and belly. Tortoises have a tough, warty covering on their head and legs.

Reptile skin does three main jobs. It keeps water out, body moisture in, and protects the creature's inside parts from injury during fights or attacks.

Spines and crests

Many reptiles have rough scales that rise into spiky points along their back. The sharp spines are good for defence. They often form beautiful crests, which are also useful for attracting a **mate**.

gecko (a lizard)

Old skin, new skin

To get rid of older, worn-out scales, all reptiles shed their outer layer of skin from time to time. This is called moulting or sloughing. Snakes shed their whole skin in one piece, starting at the head end.

This armoured spiny lizard has spiky scales along the full length of its back.

Reptile file

● A reptile's outer scales are mostly made of a material called keratin. Human hair and fingernails are also made of keratin.

● Lizards lose their skin bit by bit as it falls off in large flakes. Some peel it off with their mouth and eat it as food.

5

Sssenses

Most reptiles can see, hear and smell, but they also have other ways of detecting things. Some reptiles rely on one sense that is very well-developed, while others use a mixture of sense skills.

heat pit

emerald tree boa

Feeling the heat

Some snakes have special gaps around their lips that are sensitive to heat. These are called heat pits. They are used to detect warm-blooded animal **prey**.

Reptile file

● Snakes do not have ears on the outside. They "hear" vibrations that travel through their jaw bones and into their inner ears.

● Chameleons can move each of their eyes on its own, without moving the other. They can look in two different directions at the same time.

Fully aware

Iguanas have very clear sight and full-colour vision. Like most lizards, they detect sounds in the air using an eardrum in the skin behind the eye.

The taste test

A snake's tongue flicks in and out to collect chemicals in the air. A **sense organ** inside the mouth "smells" and "tastes" the chemicals. This helps the snake to sample food, find a mate, and to detect prey or enemies.

The snake can sense the rat's body heat, a bit like a heat-detecting camera.

The senses snakes use most are smell, taste and touch.

thin, flexible eardrum

Reptile realms

Reptiles are found in almost every part of the world, except for the Arctic and Antarctic. They are more common in hot, lowland areas than in cooler, highland regions.

Pretty dangerous

Venomous eyelash pit vipers live in the rainforests of Central and South America. The raised scales around their big, bulging eyes make them look like they have long, pretty eyelashes.

Reptile file

● Over time, many reptiles have adapted to life in villages, towns and cities.

● Moving around in hot, dry areas uses up a lot of water and energy, so desert reptiles are mainly active at night.

● Mountain peaks and polar regions are the only places without reptiles.

Sun worshippers

Most lizards are well-**adapted** to hot, dry conditions. Agama lizards make their homes in the grasslands or scrublands of Africa, where they can sun themselves to heat their bodies.

Tree boas hang down head-first ...

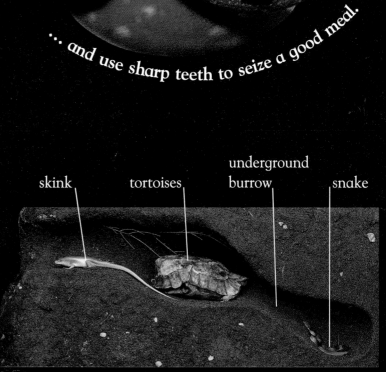

strong, gripping tail

Coiled climber

Tree boas are good climbers, with a tail that grips and holds branches tightly. Their long, slim bodies can slide easily through the branches, because they are longer and slimmer than ground boas.

... and use sharp teeth to seize a good meal.

Housemates

Many reptiles use underground burrows. Tortoises use them to escape hot, dry weather. Skinks use them to escape from **predators**. Snakes use them to hunt for prey.

skink   tortoises   underground burrow   snake

Slither slither

Snakes do not have hands and feet. Instead, they have a bendy body, which they use to wriggle and crawl over land, and swim through water. Their scales help them to grip surfaces.

Stretch marks

A snake's skeleton is simply a skull and a long, flexible backbone with ribs attached. Muscles joined to the ribs allow the snake to twist and coil its long body.

Worried rattlesnakes raise their tails..

"Buzz" off

The western diamondback rattlesnake has a venomous bite, but it does not like to waste its **venom**. It always uses its rattle first, hoping that the sound will scare off its enemy.

rattle

Don't eat me!

Some snakes have colouring that helps them to hide. Others, like the milksnake (below), have bright colours that send a message to predators. The milksnake is harmless, but has the same colouring as the venomous coral snake (right). Predators are confused, so don't attack.

...and twitch the tip to rattle out a warning "buzz".

coral snake

milksnake

Rubber-necks

Many snakes eat hard-shelled birds' eggs or soft-shelled reptile eggs. The African egg-eating snake can unhook its jaws to swallow birds' eggs that are twice the size of its head.

unhooked jaws

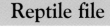

11

Lizard lunch

Most lizards are swift, **agile** predators that feed on small animals, such as insects, mammals, birds and other reptiles. Only a very small number of lizards, including large iguanas and skinks, snack on plants.

A sticky end

Chameleons are mainly insect-hunters. Their tongues are very muscular and can shoot out in a split second. A sticky tip at the end grabs, holds on to, and then pulls in the prey.

A chameleon's tongue is as long as the rest of its body.

Ah, meat!

The tegu lizard eats young birds, mammals, and even other reptiles, such as rattlesnakes.

Crunch time

Once it has caught hold of an insect, the eyed lizard stuns its prey by shaking it violently from side to side. It then passes the insect to the back of its mouth, snaps its jaws together, and crushes the prey to bits.

A chameleon's tongue is sticky to trap insects.

Keen on greens

A prickly cactus may not seem like the tastiest snack, but the Galápagos land iguana is very fond of the fleshy stems and fruits of cactus plants. The plant's sharp spines pass through the iguana's insides without harming it.

13

Enter the dragons

In the world of reptiles, dragons really do exist! These types of lizard often have incredible features that make them just as strange as the creatures found in fairy stories.

Weird beard

This bearded dragon has a set of spiky scales around its throat, a bit like a man's beard. The "beard" expands so that the lizard looks too big for predators to swallow.

What a frill!

If in danger, the frilled lizard opens its mouth wide and spreads out an umbrella-like frill around its neck. This scares away predators.

spiky beard

umbrella-like frill

Reptile file

- The eastern water dragon of Australia escapes from its enemies by diving underwater, where it can stay for up to 30 minutes.

- The frilled lizard's bright cape is a large flap of loose skin. When opened out, it can be more than four times the width of the lizard's body.

- Most lizards get around on four legs, but the crested water dragon can run on two legs when making a quick escape.

The lizard king

Komodo dragons are the largest of all living lizards, and can grow to lengths of nearly 3 metres. They can catch and kill goats and pigs, but often feed on dead animals.

Poisonous personalities

Some reptiles are "venomous". This means they can produce a poisonous liquid called venom to use for hunting or defence. A reptile's venom can **paralyse** its prey or break down its body to make it easy to eat.

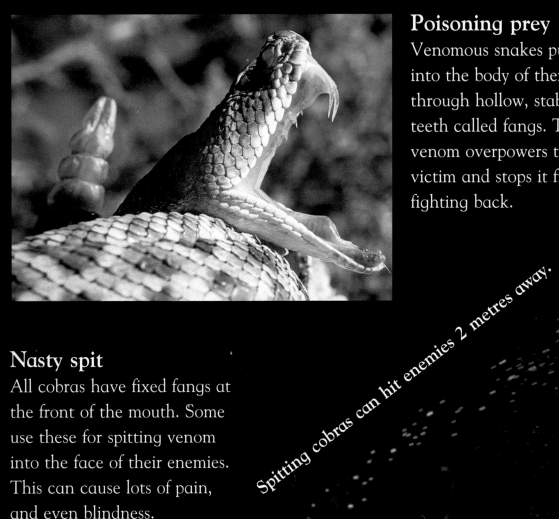

Poisoning prey

Venomous snakes put venom into the body of their prey through hollow, stabbing teeth called fangs. The venom overpowers the victim and stops it from fighting back.

Spitting cobras can hit enemies 2 metres away.

Nasty spit

All cobras have fixed fangs at the front of the mouth. Some use these for spitting venom into the face of their enemies. This can cause lots of pain, and even blindness.

venomous spit

Fold-away fangs

Vipers have extra-long, hinged fangs that can be folded away when they are not needed. After stabbing their prey with their venomous fangs, vipers "walk" their jaws from side to side over the victim to eat it.

folding fangs

Vipers can move their folding fangs one at a time, like human fingers.

THE MONSTER MUNCH

The Gila monster has venom **glands** in its lower jaw. It fools its prey by moving quite slowly until it is ready to strike. When it attacks, it turns very quickly and bites down violently. As it chews, the venom flows down grooves in its teeth and helps to kill its prey.

Venomous lizards

There are only two species of venomous lizard – the beaded lizard and the Gila (say "heela") monster. Large rodents are their biggest prey.

Gila monster

17

Leaps and bounds

Today, flying reptiles with flapping wings no longer exist. However, a few remarkable reptiles can glide long distances through the air. Many reptiles can swim, but there is one that can walk on water!

Leaping lizards

Flying geckos have webbed toes and extra flaps of skin along the head, arms, legs, sides and tail. As they jump from trees, the flaps spread out like parachutes. This slows the gecko into a graceful glide.

The gecko spreads its webbed toes as wide as possible for gliding.

The magician

The basilisk can escape danger by running across water. Its wide feet and broad, scaly toes help to keep it on top of the water. But the real trick is speed – if it goes too slowly, it will sink!

Free-falling

A flying snake
cannot actually fly,
but it can glide long
distances from tree to tree.
It steers by twisting its body
and tail and cushions its fall by
trapping a layer of air in its belly.

Flying snakes can drop right out of the danger zone.

Ready for take-off

Flying dragons live in the
rainforests of Southeast Asia
where they leap from tree to
tree. They have a fine pair of
colourful "wings", which they
lift up when ready to glide.

The hardbacks

The group of reptiles known as Chelonians all have a hard-shell home that they carry around on their back. Reptiles in this group have a set of tough features that help them to cope with their natural environments.

domed shell

Island wonder

The giant tortoises of the Galápagos Islands are not bothered by the hot, dry conditions there. They live on bare, rocky ground and can go without food and water for long periods of time.

Hard house

The shells of tortoises and turtles have a dome-shaped top, with a flatter shield under the belly. Both parts are made up of bony plates. The surface of the shell is covered in large scales called "scutes".

European pond turtle

Bottoms up!

Turtles push their head above water to take in air, but can also breathe underwater. They do this by taking air in through their skin, the lining of their throat, and also through a small hole near their bottom! Some turtles can survive for weeks underwater without having to come up for air.

Heads up!

Most turtles and tortoises have long necks to reach up and eat plants. They can also pull their heads back into their shells for protection. If they have a fight, they bring their heads right out to show their anger.

long neck

shielded belly

Shell suits

High-arched and knobbly shells give protection from bad weather and predators. Shells that blend into the natural surroundings can also help to **camouflage** tortoises and turtles.

snake-neck turtle

starred tortoise

alligator snapping turtle

terrapin

21

Sea monsters

Many reptiles are suited to ocean life. Some have powerful hearts that help them to make deep dives in cold water, and glands to remove sea salt from their bodies.

The wetter the better

Sea snakes have a flattened tail, which they use as a paddle for moving in water – a bit like a boat's oar.

flipper-shaped front legs for gliding

back feet for steering

Slick and quick

Green sea turtles have large front flippers and light, flat, smoothly-shaped shells. These features help them to move quickly through water. Some can reach speeds of up to 29 kilometres per hour.

Tough at the top

Most turtles have hard, plated shells on their backs, but the giant leatherback turtle is different. It has a tough-looking shell made of thick, leathery skin.

Reptile file

● Sea snakes are the most poisonous snakes in the world.

● Sea turtles cry salty tears. This is to get rid of the extra, unwanted salt they swallow as they swim and feed.

● The leatherback turtle can grow to 1.8 metres in length.

Seaweed feeding

The marine iguana of the Galápagos Islands is the only lizard in the world that swims and feeds in the sea. Other sea creatures need not be afraid, though, as this monster of the deep is a vegetarian. It only eats seaweed.

The marine iguana likes to sunbathe on rocks between visits to the sea.

Snap

These snappy-looking creatures are large, intelligent reptiles that are well-adapted to life in the water. Crocodiles, alligators, gharials and caimans all have similar features, but there are some interesting differences too.

The strange b[ump] on a male's sn[out] is called a gha[ra]

A gharial's teeth are all the same size and shape.

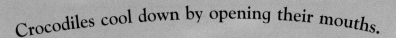

Crocodiles cool down by opening their mouths.

Nile crocodile

Snack attack

All crocodilians are **carnivores**. Even the larger crocodiles and alligators are quick and strong enough to launch themselves out of the water and snatch prey before it can run away.

Ganges gharial

Scissor-face

It is easy to recognise a gharial by the shape of its head. It has a long snout and scissor-like jaws that each contain more than 50 teeth. This kind of head is excellent for fishing.

Alligator or crocodile?

Alligators only live in the south-eastern USA and China. They have a shorter body and snout than crocodiles, but they usually live longer.

American alligator

A crocodile's fourth tooth sticks out when its mouth is closed.

Alligator junior

Caimans are a type of alligator from Central and South America. They are smaller than other crocodilians and can move much more quickly on land.

Caiman teeth are sharper than alligator teeth.

Croc characters

Reptiles in the Crocodylia group are related to
reptiles that lived more than 200 million years ago.
These relatives of the dinosaurs are fierce, dangerous
predators, but they are also surprisingly caring parents.

Ready-salted

The **saltwater** crocodile, or "saltie",
is one of the few crocs to **inhabit**
saltwater, although it also lives in
freshwater rivers and lakes. Salties
have large glands on the back of their
tongue to get rid of unwanted salt.

MONSTER OF THE DEEP

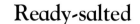

Saltwater crocodiles are the largest reptiles alive today,
and some of the world's most powerful animals.
They can stay underwater for more than an
hour, and are strong enough to kill and
eat a human. The "saltie" lives over a wide
area, from southern India to Fiji in the Pacific
Ocean, and has been seen hundreds of
kilometres from the nearest land.

Careful crocs

A female crocodile carries her newly hatched young inside her mouth. She can carry as many as 15 in one go, delivering them safely to the water. This is very important for the babies' survival.

baby crocodile

Dwarf of the riverbank

Dwarf crocodiles are the smallest species of crocodile growing to just 2 metres long. They are shy animals that hide away in riverbank holes when in danger.

Croc courtship

To attract a mate, male crocodilians lift up their heads and bellow. The noise helps to warn off rival males. They also blow bubbles in the water to win the attention of females.

dwarf crocodile

Nile crocodile

Reptile breeding

Most reptiles hatch from eggs, although some do give birth to live young. Even reptiles that live in the water usually lay their eggs on land. This is so that babies can get oxygen from the air.

Chips off the old block

Whether **hatchlings** or live young, reptile babies usually look like miniature versions of their parents. The baby leopard tortoise will develop its darker, adult markings as it grows up.

The not so great escape

Snakes lay eggs with soft, leathery shells. The hatchlings have a special "egg" tooth, which they use to tear a hole in the shell. It can take up to 2 days for a baby snake to get out of the egg.

Reptile file

- Most reptiles leave their young to look after themselves.
- Reptiles with fewer young are usually better parents.
- Marine turtles can lay as many as 200 eggs in one go.

Ready-made babies

Lots of snakes and lizards give birth to live young. Lizards and snakes that hatch inside the body of their mother usually have a greater chance of survival.

Safety in the sea

Female turtles make nests in the sand using their back flippers. They lay very large **clutches** of eggs. Once hatched, the young turtles make their way directly to the sea. Here, they will be less at risk from attack.

hatching
turtle

Meet the relatives

Reptiles have a long history – their relatives have been around since the days of the dinosaurs. Crocodiles are the closest-living relatives of the dinosaurs, but they were not the first reptiles to inhabit our world. **Fossils** show that the distant relatives of turtles may have been around at the same time as the very first dinosaurs.

third eye

Eye of the tuatara
Like many lizards, tuataras have a mysterious third eye under the skin on their forehead. It is not used for seeing things above them, but it can detect strong light and colour.

LAST OF THE BEAK-HEADS

During the age of the dinosaurs, there were many "beak-head" reptiles. Today the tuatara is the only creature of this species left.

Evolution

There were once many
flying, bat-like reptiles
called pterosaurs (say "terra-
saws"). Like bats, they
had wings made of
skin stretched
between
their finger
bones. Some
of today's reptiles, such as
crocodiles, are related to birds.
Of all living reptiles, snakes
were the last to appear.

pterosaur

Tuataras can live to be 120 years old.

Glossary

adapted changed over time to become suited to a certain habitat or environment

agile can move quickly and easily

bask lie in the sun

camouflage hide or disguise

carnivores meat-eaters

clutches groups of eggs all laid at the same time

digest break down food in stomach

fossils remains of ancient animal or plant preserved in rock

freshwater water areas that are not salty, such as ponds and rivers

glands body parts that squeeze out things such as sweat, salt or venom

hatchlings baby animals that are born from eggs

inhabit live in

mate partner to breed (have babies) with

moisture wetness

paralyse make unable to move

predator animal that hunts other animals for food

prey animals that are hunted for food

saltwater water areas that are salty, such as seas and oceans

sense organ body part that can detect something, such as light, sound, vibrations, texture, temperature, electrical signals, smells or tastes

species group of animals or plants made up of similar individuals

venom poison

venomous has poisonous venom

Index